100 EASY
TALK
THOUGHTS
FOR YOUTH
LDS
VOLUME ONE

100 EASY TALK THOUGHTS FOR LDS YOUTH

VOLUME ONE

Sandra & Joseph Harper

ISBN: 1-55517-417-5
v.6

Published by: **Bonneville Books**

Distributed by:

925 North Main, Springville, UT 84663 • 801/489-4084

CFI | Publishing and Distribution Since 1986

Cedar Fort, Incorporated

CFI Distribution • CFI Books • Council Press • Bonneville Books

Cover design by Corinne A. Bischoff and Sheila Mortimer
Printed in the United States of America

Wisdom is the principle thing,
Therefore get wisdom: and with all thy
getting get understanding. "

Proverbs 4:7

A definition for the word *principle* in the context that this volume will use it is found in Webster's dictionary as follows: "A fundamental truth; a primary law, or doctrine."

ACKNOWLEDGMENTS

We need to thank two very special and talented women for their services: Jackie Wynder, our first editor, waded through the raw beginnings of this work and gave encouragement as well as expert suggestions; and Jennifer Barker, our final editor, rendered the professional quality found in the final copy.

INTRODUCTION

This book is written with the intent to answer questions that are frequently asked, but seldom fully answered with scriptures.

Each chapter is opened with a question that I personally have heard asked by someone.

In this work I have opened a study that will answer these questions with the most precious insights of the gospel. It is meant to make the gospel a more adaptable and enjoyable part of our lives.

There is no end to learning, so it would be best to enjoy the learning process.

I have found that my greatest enjoyment in learning the gospel comes in the discovery that it's simply common sense.

Also, seeing the purpose of all the symbolism, and the interdependence of each principle as it builds like a *tree* truly piques my excitement.

Like the tree there is a central trunk from which everything else extends. This trunk is Christ.

When we start with Christ in each of the gospel teachings we find how they all connect into one simple formula for life.

Part One
THE GROUNDWORK

WHAT IS TRUTH?

WHAT ARE THE LIGHT AND SPIRIT OF JESUS CHRIST AND THE HOLY GHOST?

WHY THE MYSTERY?

&cᴣ

WHAT IS TRUTH?

———◆———

A sister once made the familiar comment that "You can prove anything with the scriptures." It is true. But why are the scriptures so often interpreted differently even within our own Church?"

A mandate for salvation is "understanding" the requirements. So how can we know what is really true and what is just an individual's interpretation?

Thought One
FINDING TRUTH

2 Peter 1:20-21 says:

> Knowing this first, that no prophecy of the scripture is of any private interpretation. For the prophecy came not in old time by the will of man: but holy men of God spake as they were moved by the Holy Ghost.

Today, more than any other time in our history, truth is difficult to discern. Cunning phrasing, impressive endorsements, and artful use of authoritative scriptures all can leave us a bit confused or led down the wrong path. Ephesians 4:14 &18 says:

> That we henceforth be no more children, tossed to and fro, and carried about with every wind of doctrine, by the sleight of men, and cunning craftiness, whereby they lie in wait to deceive;...Having the understanding darkened, being alienated from the life of God through the ignorance that is in them, because of the blindness of their heart;

So how can we know what is really true and what is just an individual's interpretation?

Thought Two
THE GIFT OF THE HOLY GHOST

With the confusion about what is truth we can realize why the Lord saw fit to give us the "gift of the Holy Ghost."

It isn't sufficient to just have the Holy Ghost now and again, it is absolutely essential that we have his guidance at every turn in our lives.

If we are not righteous, warranting his constant companionship in our walk through life, we may fail. 2 Nephi 33:2 says:

> But behold, there are many that harden their hearts against the Holy Spirit, that it hath no place in them; wherefore, they cast many things away which are written and esteem them as things of naught.

We may cast important things away without the "Spirit's" constant guidance.

Thought Three
PRAY FOR GUIDANCE

When we are being taught from the scriptures, it's very easy to just whisper a silent prayer in our hearts and ask if we are really being given the correct interpretation. Moroni 10:4-5 says:

> And when ye shall receive these things, I would exhort you that ye would ask God, the Eternal Father, in the name of Christ, if these things are not true; and if ye shall ask with a sincere heart, with real intent, having faith in Christ, he will manifest the truth of it unto you by the power of the Holy Ghost.

The next verse goes on to say that by the power of the Holy Ghost ye may know the truth of *all* things.

Thought Four
IS IT JUST AND TRUE?

Moroni also gives us a very important piece of information to help us discern truth. Moroni 10:6 says:

> And whatsoever thing is good is *just and true;* wherefore, nothing that is good denieth the Christ, but acknowledgeth that he is.

Whatsoever thing is good is *just and true.* That is a powerful observation. Think about it for a moment.

He gives us even more by saying that nothing good or just and true denieth the Christ.

If we apply this insight into our study or learning by asking if what we are reading or hearing teaches of Christ or is just and true, then very little if anything will be able to slip by us which is not good.

3

Thought Five
CAN WE TRUST TO OTHERS?

Always relying on and expecting others to teach us is spiritually dangerous for both them and us. Everyone is a sinner. 1 John 1:8 says:

> If we say that we have no sin, we deceive ourselves, and the truth is not in us.

Everyone makes errors.

It is well to be as the wise virgins found in Christ's parable of the Ten Virgins and carry our own oil, not hoping for borrowed light. Matthew 25:4&8 says:

> But the wise took oil in their vessels with their lamps…And the foolish said unto the wise, Give us of your oil; for our lamps are gone out.

Gaining our own light by studying with the Spirit is the safest way. Not to mention, depending on borrowed light is slothful and unwise.

Thought Six
WISE AND NOT SLOTHFUL

We will be prepared to see error when it presents itself as we are wise and not slothful servants. D&C 58:26 says:

> For behold, it is not meet that I should command in all things; for he that is compelled in all things, the same is a slothful and not a wise servant; wherefore he receiveth no reward.

In other words, it is wise to do our own study of all the principles and truths of the gospel with the Holy Ghost beforehand.

We are constantly encouraged to gain knowledge about those who are seeking public office, to become informed about their platforms.

Given the grand purpose of our lives on this earth, it is more important to gain as much knowledge as possible of our Father in Heaven and His Son Jesus Christ; and become informed of their gospel and work for our salvation.

Section Two

WHAT ARE THE LIGHT AND SPIRIT OF JESUS CHRIST AND THE HOLY GHOST?

In Sacrament meeting the topic spoken on was the Holy Ghost. During the process of the talk, the speaker used several scriptures that referred to the Spirit of Jesus Christ and the Light of Christ as if they were interchangeable with the Holy Ghost. Are all three the same thing? If not, what is their relationship to each other?

Thought Seven
SPIRITUAL FACILITATORS

There are three spiritual facilitators from which we may gain understanding, guidance, and truth.

These are the *Light of Christ* or conscience, *The Spirit of Christ* or Spirit of the Lord or Spirit of Truth when referring to the Second Comforter, and the *Holy Ghost* called the Spirit of God, who, when received as the Gift of the Holy Ghost is the First Comforter. These are just the most prominent names.

Though they have several separate functions and titles, they come from only two distinct and separate beings; Jesus Christ and the Holy Ghost. The first Article of Faith teaches the separateness of these two. It says:

> We believe in God, the Eternal Father, and in His son, Jesus Christ, and in the Holy Ghost.

They can most easily be identified by what they are doing at any given time. It is like a father and mother of a family who are also a husband and wife, and both Doctors. One of medicine and one of Philosophy.

When they are doing things as parents, they are called parents or father and mother. When they are doing things as a husband or wife or individuals, they will then be called by name or title such as Jim, Doris, or Mr. and Mrs. But if they are doing things as Doctors, then they both will carry the same title; Doctor, but are not the same nor will they attempt to do each others jobs.

Though they each have several titles, some of which are the same, they are still just two, but completely different people with different duties.

Thought Eight
WHAT IS THE LIGHT OF CHRIST?

The Light of Christ is the first spiritual facilitator we receive. John 1:9 says:

That was the true Light, which lighteth every man that cometh into the world.

The spark that kindles life into each of us is the Light of Christ which is given to everyone who is born into the world. Also D&C 88:50 says:

Then shall ye know that ye have seen me, that I am, and that I am the true light that is in you, and that you are in me; otherwise ye could not abound.

Refer to D&C 88:6-13 , John 1:1-5, and Acts 17:27-28 for further clarification.

It is like a spiritual heart beating life into each of us in order that we may abound or live in this physical world and have the ability to access the guidance of the spiritual realm through the Holy Ghost and the Spirit of Christ.

It is sometimes referred to as the conscience. In simple terms, it is the power for our spirits to exist and receive spiritual guidance in a physical world.

Thought Nine
WHAT IS THE SPIRIT OF JESUS CHRIST?

Just as our spirits are intelligences of truth and light, the Spirit of Jesus Christ is also. D&C 84:45 says:

For the word of the Lord is truth, and whatsoever is truth is light, and whatsoever is light is spirit, even the Spirit of Jesus Christ.

When we received the spiritual heart or light of Christ, it was the power of life He shared with each one of us so that we could simultaneously exist *physically* and *spiritually* in order to increase in our own light and intelligence.

The prayers of the righteous are answered by the Spirit of Christ. When the brother of Jared received his answer to prayer concerning the lighting of the ships, it was the Spirit of Christ which answered him. Ether 3:16 says:

Behold, this body, which ye now behold, is the body of my spirit; and man have I created after the body of my spirit; and even as I appear unto thee to be in the spirit will I appear unto my people in the flesh.

This took place when Jesus was a pre-mortal being, but even after He received His resurrected body, He could still dwell in us the same way as the rays of the sun can be in a room, giving warmth and light, without the actual body of the Sun being in that room. Ephesians 3:17 says:

That Christ may dwell in you hearts by faith...

We receive the Spirit of Christ facilitated by the Holy Ghost through the light of Christ. However, we must be righteous or holy. Helaman 4:24 says:

And they saw that they had become weak, like unto their brethren, the Lamanites, and that the Spirit of the Lord did no more preserve them; yea, it had withdrawn from them because the Spirit of the Lord doth not dwell in unholy temples—

Thought Ten

THE SPIRIT OF JESUS CHRIST AND THE HOLY GHOST

The Spirit of Jesus Christ and the Holy Ghost are often mistaken for each other since they have so much in common.

First, both the *Spirit of Christ* and the *Holy Ghost* are referred to as the *Spirit*. This because the *Holy Ghost* is referred to on occasion as the *Spirit of God*. Second, they are both Comforters. The Holy Ghost is the First Comforter. John 14:26 says:

But the Comforter, which is the Holy Ghost, whom the Father will send in my name, he shall teach you all things, and bring to your remembrance, whatsoever I have said unto you.

The Spirit of Christ is the Second Comforter and called the *Spirit of Truth* at such times. John 14:16-17 says:

And I will pray the Father, and he shall give you another Comforter, that he may abide with you forever; Even the Spirit of truth; whom the world cannot receive, because it seeth him not, neither knoweth him: but ye know him; for he dwelleth with you, and shall be in you.

The third reason they are confused is the *Holy Ghost* must be present in order for *The Spirit of Jesus Christ* to work among us. Ezekiel 2:2 says:

And the spirit (the Holy Ghost) entered into me when he (The Spirit of Christ) spake unto me, and stood me upon my feet, that I heard him that spake unto me.

The Holy Ghost entered into him and stood him on his feet when *The Spirit of Christ* spoke to him so that he could hear *The Spirit of Christ* speak.

Since only Christ can take away our sins, it is the Spirit of Christ that cleanses our spirits through the Holy Ghost after we have repented. Moses 6:65 says:

...And thus he was baptized, and the Spirit of God descended upon him, and thus he was born of the Spirit, and became quickened in the inner man...Thou are baptized with fire, and with the Holy Ghost...

The descending of the Spirit of God upon us is the Holy Ghost and the baptism by fire is the Spirit of Jesus Christ.

When the Holy Ghost enters, we are filled with light, becoming cleansed by the Spirit of Christ, or fire, which upon entering, quickens our inner person or spirit and we become cleansed.

Thought Eleven

WHAT IS THE HOLY GHOST?

It is a spirit only. D&C 130:22 says in part:

...the Holy Ghost has not a body of flesh and bones, but is a personage of Spirit. Were it not so, the Holy Ghost could not dwell in us.

The *Holy Ghost* is like the mediator of the spiritual heart and is the one that accesses and prepares each of us for *The Spirit of Christ* to enter.

Since only Christ can take away our sins, it is *The Spirit of Christ* that cleanses us, but only through the *Holy Ghost*, after we have repented. Moses 6:65 says in part:

> And thus he was baptized, and the Spirit of God descended upon him, and thus he was born of the Spirit, and became quickened in the inner man...Thou art baptized with fire, and with the Holy Ghost...

The descending of the Spirit of God upon us is the Ghost and the baptism by fire is the Spirit of Christ.

When the *Holy Ghost* descends upon us, the *Spirit of Christ or fire* can then enter, and upon entering, quickens our inner person or spirit and we become cleansed as by fire.

The Holy Ghost is also to confirm and teach truth. John 14:26 says:

> But the Comforter, which is the Holy Ghost, whom the Father will send in my name, he shall teach you all things, and bring all things to your remembrance, whatsoever I have said unto you.

The *Holy Ghost* can bring to our remembrance things we have been taught. He can also teach us new things pertaining to gospel principles, but he cannot personally give us answers for our problems or bless us. This responsibility is only for *The Spirit of Christ.*

Thought Twelve
HOW DO THEY WORK TOGETHER?

Imagine the Light of Christ, as a light inside of each of us. When the light of the Holy Ghost is added to it, the brightness of the light increases.

As long as the Holy Ghost is present, the light is increased, not only through the addition of his own light, but by acting as a reflective enhancer of the Light of Christ.

A story of Thomas Edison gives us a little idea of how they work together.

When Thomas Edison was a young boy, his mother had an appendicitis attack. In those days there were no lights except for the not so bright coal oil lamps, so an appendicitis attack was fatal if it happened at night.

The doctor told the boy that his mother would die without an operation, but that it was too dark to perform it.

When Thomas heard this, he came up with an idea of putting all of the lamps available into one room. However it still was not enough. He then thought of surrounding those lights with mirrors to further enhance their light. This he did and the operation was successfully performed.

The Light of Christ within each of us can be *enhanced* by the Holy Ghost as Thomas Edison enhanced the coal oil lamps with mirrors.

Thought Thirteen
MORE SOURCES

The Holy Ghost is also referred to as the Spirit of God.

1. Scriptures defining the Holy Ghost as the Spirit of God:

a. Matthew 3:16 says:

And Jesus, when he was baptized, went up straightway out of the water: and, lo, the heavens were opened unto him, and he saw the Spirit of God descending like a dove, and lighting upon him:

b. 2 Nephi 31:8 says:

Wherefore, after he was baptized with water the Holy Ghost descended upon him in the form of a dove.

The footnote on John 16:13 in our scriptures calls the Spirit of truth the conscience, but with the other references from John 14:16 and D&C 93:26, it is actually the Second Comforter.

Though the Second Comforter is Christ, the difference between the conscience, which is one of the functions of the Light of Christ, and the Second Comforter is the same as the difference between the Holy Ghost and the Gift of the Holy Ghost.

The Teachings of the Prophet Joseph Smith teaches us the difference between the First and Second Comforters. Pages 150-151 says:

> The other Comforter spoken of is a subject of great interest, and perhaps understood by few of this generation. After a person has faith in Christ, repents of his sins, and is baptized for the remission of his sins and receives the Holy Ghost, (by the laying on of hands), which is the first Comforter, then let him continue to humble himself before God, hungering and thirsting after righteousness, and living by every word of God, and the Lord will soon say unto him, Son, thou shalt be exalted. When the Lord has thoroughly proved him, and finds that the man is determined to serve Him at all hazards, then the man will find his calling and his election made sure, then it will be his privilege to receive the other comforter, which the Lord hath promised the Saints, as is recorded in the testimony of St. John, in the 14th chapter, from the 12th to the 27th verses.

Note the 16, 17, 18, and 23 verses:

> 16 And I will pray the Father, and *He shall give you another Comforter, that he may abide with you forever:*
>
> 17 *Even the Spirit of Truth; whom the world cannot receive, because it seeth him not, neither knoweth him; but ye know him, for he dwelleth with you, and shall be in you.*
>
> 18 I will not leave you comfortless: *I will come to you.*
>
> 21 *He that hath my commandments, and keepeth them, he it is that loveth me: and he tat loveth me shall be love of my Father and I will love him, and will manifest myself to him.*
>
> 23 If a man love me, he will keep my word: and my Father will love him, and *we will come unto him, and make our abode with him.*

Now what is the other Comforter? It is no more nor less than the Lord Jesus Christ Himself: and this is the sum and substance of the whole matter: that when any man obtains this last Comforter, he will have the personage of Jesus Christ to attend him, or appear unto him from time to time, and even He will manifest the Father unto him, and they will take up their abode with him, and visions of the heavens will be opened unto him, and the Lord will teach him face to face, and he my have a perfect knowledge of the mysteries of the kingdom of God; and this is the estate and place the ancient Saints arrived at when they had glorious visions — Isaiah, Ezekiel, John upon the Isle of Patmos, St. Paul in the three heavens, and ALL THE SAINTS who held communion with the general assembly and Church of the Firstborn (Teachings of the Prophet Joseph Smith).

❦

WHY THE MYSTERY?

—◆—

*A young man asked where God began
and why did He have a religious and
not a common sense approach to eternal
life? He was told that these were
mysteries and not to worry about them.
It wasn't necessary for him to know.*

Thought Fourteen

SHOULD WE DELVE INTO THE MYSTERIES?

Some have said in the past that we are not to delve into the mysteries, that anything we don't understand should be left alone. What is the Lord's desire for us?

In the 42nd section of the D&C verse 61 says that if we ask, we will be given to know the mysteries.

> If thou shalt ask, thou shalt receive revelation upon revelation, knowledge upon knowledge, that thou mayest know the mysteries and the peaceable things—that which bringeth joy, that which bringeth life eternal.

Yes we should delve into the gospel mysteries. They are where a wealth of joy is hidden.

———◆———

Thought Fifteen

SEARCH, PONDER AND PRAY

We are taught to search, ponder and pray in order to understand and learn as much as we can. John 5:39 says:

> Search the scriptures; for in them ye think ye have eternal life: and they are they which testify of me.

Also 3 Nephi 17:3 which says:

> Therefore, go ye unto your homes, and ponder upon the things which I have said, and ask of the Father, in my name, that ye may understand, and prepare your minds for the morrow, and I come unto you again.

Searching out, pondering on, and praying about the things we don't understand is not only right, but our responsibility.

———◆———

WHY THE MYSTERY?

1 Corinthians 2:7 says:

> But we speak the wisdom of God in a mystery, even the hidden wisdom, which God ordained before the world unto our glory:

Why is our religion full of mysteries about our God and His knowledge?

When we read a mystery, do we not "hunger and thirst" to know and understand the workings behind the story? Matthew 5:6 says:

> Blessed are they which do hunger and thirst after righteousness: for they shall be filled.

It is God's way of causing a hunger and thirst within us that will bring us in search of Him and His ways. 1 Corinthians 2:10-11 says:

> But God hath revealed them unto us by his Spirit: for the Spirit searcheth all things, yea, the deep things of God...even so the things of God knoweth no man, but (by) the Spirit of God.

By making the gospel a mystery, we are given only what we are prepared to receive.

Thought Seventeen
PREPARE TO RECEIVE

The searching spirit's "hungering and thirsting" is part of the preparation for receiving greater knowledge and understanding. 2 Nephi 28:30 says:

> For behold, thus saith the Lord God: I will give unto the children of men line upon line, precept upon precept, here a little and there a little; and blessed are these who hearken unto my precepts, and lend an ear unto my counsel, for they shall learn wisdom; for unto him that receiveth I will give more;...

We are God's children. In all His ways, He deals with us as children; giving only what we are ready to accept and then as we increase in readiness He gives us more.

He knows that as children He must first get our interest. Making this life a mysterious treasure hunt, can pique our interests and be the motivation to keep learning and seeking more.

WHAT IS THE GLORY OF GOD?

A young woman stated that she knew she was a child of God from a pre-existence in Heaven, and was to try and become like her Father in Heaven who is perfect. But what she didn't understand was who and what her Heavenly Father is and what on this earth works for becoming like Him.

WHO ARE WE REALLY?

Our search for understanding starts with learning our identity. Abraham 3:22 says:

> Now the Lord had shown unto me, Abraham, the intelligences that were organized before the world was;…

We are intelligences. Understanding what being an intelligence is, gives us our divine identity as well as our relationship to God.

In the D&C 93:36 we learn that:

> The glory of God is intelligence, or in other words, light and truth…

As intelligences we are part of God's glory, or truth and light. D&C 93:29 says:

> Man was also in the beginning with God. Intelligence, or the light of truth, was not created or made, neither indeed can be.

We were not created or made, but organized. We are as eternal as God, for we are part of Him. As such, we can progress eternally, gaining greater and greater glory as He does.

WE ARE HIS CHILDREN

We are part of God or His offspring. Acts 17:28 says:

> For in him we live, and move, and have our being; as certain also of your poets have said, For we are also his offspring.

As offsprings of God, we are gods in the making. With this in mind, we should truly desire and seek to do all that is asked of us by the Father. And what does He ask? Matthew 5:48 says:

> Be ye therefore perfect, even as your Father which is in heaven is perfect.

God wants us to become like him. We are His literal sons and daughters. D&C 76:24 & 58 says:

...and the inhabitants thereof are begotten sons and daughters unto God...Wherefore, as it is written, they are gods, even the sons of God—

So it is not only our potential but His work as a parent. Moses 1:39 says:

For behold, this is my work and my glory—to bring to pass the immortality and eternal life of man.

WHAT MAKES LIFE A TEST?

Abraham 3:24-25 says:

And there stood one among them that was like unto God, and he said unto those who were with him: We will go down, for there is space there, and we will take of these materials, and we will make an earth whereon these may dwell; And we will prove them herewith, to see if they will do all things whatsoever the Lord their God shall command them;

We prove ourselves by finding God, the Father of our Spirits, and instructing and establishing ourselves again in His word and Spirit while in this totally physical world.

What makes it a test is not knowing or being known like we were in the pre-existence. 1 Corinthians 13:12 says:

For now we see through a glass, darkly; but then face to face: now I know in part; but then shall I know even as also I am known.

While we're here on earth, we see as through a glass; darkly; or rather we have a veil placed between us and the heavens, preventing us from remembering our pre-existence.

Not seeing things from an eternal perspective is the reason we will only know things in part.

But when we are face to face with God, we shall not only know all, but shall be known by all.

Thought Twenty-one

ARE WE THE ONLY ONES?

God organized our intelligences and created a world where we could be tested, or furthered in our progress.

It wasn't the first time. He has done this many times. Moses 1:33-34 says:

> And worlds without number have I created; and I also created them for mine own purpose; and by the Son I created them, which is mine Only Begotten. And the first man of all men have I called Adam, which is many.

This is the eternal progression of God, to create worlds without number for His organized intelligences or offspring to increase.

———

Thought Twenty-two

WE EITHER INCREASE OR DECREASE

Think about the outcome of the parable of the talents. Matthew 25:15-21 records this parable.

> And unto one he gave five talents, to another two, and to another one;…Then he that had received the five talents went and traded with the same, and made them other five talents. And likewise he that had received two, he also gained other two. But he that had received one went and digged in the earth, and hid his lord's money. After a long time the lord of those servants cometh, and reckoneth with them.

The Lord was pleased with the first two servants who increased their talents.

"His lord said unto him, Well done, thou good and faithful servant; thou hast been faithful over a few things, I will make thee ruler over many things: enter thou into the joy of thy lord."

But the one that received one talent, and buried it, had quite a different fate. Matthew 25:24-28 says:

Then he which had received the one talent came and said, lord,...I was afraid, and went and hid thy talent in the earth: Lo, there thou hast that is thine. His lord answered and said unto him, Thou wicked and slothful servant,...Take therefore the talent from him, and give it unto him which hath ten talents.

We can't progress by burying our intelligence or glory.

Thought Twenty-three
OBEDIENCE IS PROGRESS

Just as water is stopped from moving forward by a "dam," our spiritual progression can be stopped or damned by our lack of obedience.

Not progressing is the same as being damned.

Obedience increases our intelligence and glorifies us in truth. We receive more truth and light until we have a fullness. D&C 93:26-28 says:

> The Spirit of truth is of God. I am the Spirit of truth, and John bore record of me, saying: He received a fullness of truth, yea, even of all truth; And no man receiveth a fullness unless he keepeth his commandments. He that keepeth his commandments receiveth truth and light, until he is glorified in truth and knoweth all things.

So we gain a fullness which is receiving of glory, or being glorified. We can receive more glory or intelligence and progress, but only by obedience.

Thought Twenty-four
OBEDIENCE NEEDS AGENCY

In order to obey and increase in intelligence, it is essential we have free agency.

It is being free to make choices and suffer the consequences that we gain more knowledge and learn obedience, and by obedience increase in our intelligence.

Even the Savior learned this way. Hebrews 5:8 says:

> Though he were a Son, yet learned he obedience by the things which he suffered; And being made perfect, he became the author of eternal salvation unto all them that obey him;

We were not given agency as a whim of God, but as an eternal principle upon which not only our progress is dependent but our very existence. D&C 93:30 says:

> All truth is independent in that sphere in which God has placed it, to act for itself, as all intelligence also; otherwise there is no existence.

———

Thought Twenty-five
FREE AGENCY MUST BE GUARDED

Our very existence depends on agency, so it must be guarded at all cost—that's why we fought a war in heaven. Moses 4:3 says:

> Wherefore, because that Satan rebelled against me and sought to destroy the agency of man, which I, the Lord God, had given him, and also, that I should give unto him mine own power; by the power of mine Only Begotten, I caused that he should be cast down;

To be denied our free agency would be like us being root-bound plants, we would be unable to grow. We would wither and die.

God couldn't let us lose our free agency because it is His work and glory to make our glory increase. Moses 1:39 says:

> For behold, this is my work and my glory—to bring to pass the immortality and eternal life of man.

So with valiant struggles, and the cost of one third the host of heaven, we helped win our agency.

Thought Twenty-six
TRIALS EQUAL GLORY

As we continue to gain knowledge we discover that trials or afflictions increase our intelligence.

We will have afflictions come for different reasons, some for our own sins as chastisements, others as trials of our faith in Christ.

We know, however, that whatever the reason, they can help us gain greater glory. 2 Corinthians 4:17 says:

> For our light affliction, which is but for a moment, worketh for us a far more exceeding and eternal weight of glory;…

If we have few or no afflictions of great magnitude, we are not necessarily more blessed than those who have many. Hebrews 12:6 says:

> For whom the Lord loveth he chasteneth and scourgeth every son whom he receiveth.

Trials of this world can be blessings. We can't progress as far or gain as much intelligence or glory without them.

Growing through these trials is also necessary in order to keep our second estate. D&C 136:37 says:

> My people must be tried in all things, that they may be prepared to receive the glory that I have for them, even the glory of Zion; and he that will not hear chastisement is not worthy of my kingdom.

Thought Twenty-seven
WHY OPPOSITION?

Just as agency is necessary to our progress, opposition is too. What choice would there be, if there were only good? 2 Nephi 2:11-12 says:

For it must needs be, that there is an opposition in all things. If not so,...righteousness could not be brought to pass, neither wickedness, neither holiness nor misery, neither good nor bad. Wherefore all things must needs be a compound in one; wherefore, if it should be one body it must needs remaineth as dead, having no life neither death, nor corruption nor incorruption, happiness nor misery, neither sense nor insensibility. Wherefore, it must needs have been created for a thing of naught; wherefore there would have been no purpose in the end of its creation. Wherefore, this thing must needs destroy the wisdom of God and his eternal purposes, and also the power and the mercy, and the justice of God.

An opposing force is essential for balance to insure existence and progress.

You can't have good without evil, or light without darkness.

WHAT IS THE MAGNITUDE OF AGENCY?

A sister made the statement in a Gospel Doctrine class that it was very hard for her to allow her children their "free agency," and so she just couldn't understand how God was able to allow all of us to have our "free agency."

WHY FREE AGENCY?

God allows us our free agency because He knows that it is fundamental to our progress as an eternal principle, and that our existence depends upon it.

D&C 93:30 says:

> All truth is independent in that sphere in which God has placed it, to act for itself, as all intelligence also; otherwise there is no existence.

Truth gives us freedom. John 8:32 says:

> And ye shall know the truth, and the truth shall make you free.

Our existence depends upon agency, and agency depends upon truth.

In the pre-existence we gained freedom to continue to progress by making the correct choice to hold to truth.

Thought Twenty-nine
INSIGHT TO FREE AGENCY

Who and what we are has everything to do with free agency. First of all, we are intelligences. Abraham 3:22 says:

> Now the Lord had shown unto me, Abraham, the intelligences that were organized before the world was...

Second, intelligence is truth and light. D&C 93:36 says:

> The glory of God is intelligence, or in other words, light and truth.

We are the very essence of freedom or agency because we are truth which makes us free. John 8:32 says:

> And ye shall know the truth, and the truth shall make you free.

That is why our very existence of our beings depends on being allowed freedom.

So the glory of God or intelligence, light and truth, are free agency producing.

Thought Thirty
SATAN'S FOLLY

Satan was a competitor, and competition in it's very function is opposition.

Though competition or opposition is necessary, it can be used wrongly. 2 Nephi 2:11 says:

> For it must needs be, that there is an opposition in all things...

Though competition or opposition is necessary, it can be used wrongly.

Satan used it wrongly to oppose truth or free agency. Opposition to truth and light is ignorance and darkness.

Truth gives freedom, and ignorance produces captivity.

Because Satan established his rebellion upon ignorance, which is the opposing force to truth, he lost his own agency.

With this act he introduced the element of opposition to us and we were faced with making a choice.

In his ignorance or lack of wisdom, Satan didn't understand that our very existence depended upon our free agency.

Lacking the knowledge that without agency there is no truth, and without truth there is no intelligence, and without intelligence there is no existence, he plunged himself and a host of others into greater ignorance and captivity.

Thought Thirty-one
SATAN WANTED US

Satan rebelled against the eternal principle of free agency. Moses 4:3 says:

> ...Satan rebelled against me and sought to destroy the agency of man, which I, the Lord God, had given him...

We are glory, and the kingdom of God is a kingdom of glory.

A kingdom of glory is a kingdom of intelligence, truth and light.

Because of who and what we are, this kingdom is within each of us. Luke 17:21 says:

> Neither shall they say, Lo here! or lo there! for, behold, the kingdom of God is within you.

Satan wanted to take God's kingdom of glory which we are, away. This is what is said about Satan in D&C 76:28:

> ...for we beheld Satan, that old serpent, even the devil, who rebelled against God, and sought to take the kingdom of God and His Christ.

We are God's glory and His kingdom. Satan sought to take us and Christ away from God.

———————

Thought Thirty-two
SATAN'S PLAN BACKFIRED

Satan and the third that followed him lost their agency and physical existence because they lacked understanding of the eternal principle of agency.

The phrase found in D&C 131:6 says:

> It is impossible for a man to be saved in ignorance.

It takes on greater meaning when we understand ignorance and darkness oppose truth and light.

Ignorance is captivity and we can't be saved or progress in captivity. Where Satan and the lost one-third are, progress is impossible.

Unlike Satan, the Savior understood the significance of agency and was willing to submit to it.

He not only allowed us our agency, He sacrificed His life to pay for the mistakes we would make because of it.

Therefore, we were given to Him. John 3:35 says:

> The Father loveth the Son, and hath given all things into his hand.

Thought Thirty-three
REBELLION AND OPPRESSION

Disobedience to any principles, especially eternal ones such as agency, is rebellion.

Satan rebelled, and if we do the same we lose our free agency and become his captives.

It is Satan's desire to lead us captive and take our free agency away.

Oppression is a sin against free agency and is of Satan.

In the November 15, 1851 Volume 13 issue of the *Millennial Star* John Taylor refers to a statement given by Joseph Smith. It says: "I teach them correct principles and they govern themselves."

In other words, we are to teach and be taught truth and then allow the *freedom* gained from that truth to govern ourselves.

Thought Thirty-four
PRIESTHOOD AND FREE AGENCY

The Spirit of the Lord is truth, *meaning freedom giving—* D&C 84:45 says:

> For the word of the Lord is truth, and whatsoever is truth is light, and whatsoever is light is Spirit, even the Spirit of Jesus Christ.

His *Spirit* which is truth and light is grieved when someone in power tries to take away free agency. D&C 121:37 says in part:

> ...or to exercise control or dominion or compulsion upon the souls of the children of men, in any degree of unrighteousness, behold, the heavens withdraw themselves; the Spirit of the Lord is grieved; and when it is withdrawn, Amen to the priesthood or the authority of that man.

Truth gives freedom, and truth is light, or the Spirit of Jesus Christ.

So when our agency which is truth is taken away, the Spirit of Jesus Christ which is truth will also be withdrawn.

If the *Spirit* of Jesus Christ is not present, then neither is His *power.*

Thought Thirty-five
AGENCY AND ACCOUNTABILITY

As intelligences which are to act for ourselves, we are *free and accountable.*

When our free agency is taken, the accountability is not always lost.

Though Satan and his hosts have given up their agency, they are still accountable. Jude 1:6 says:

> And the angels which kept not their first estate, but left their own habitation, He hath reserved in everlasting chains under darkness unto the judgment of the great day.

Our accountability is not lost if we chose to follow anyone in ignorance and they lead us astray.

We must always stay alert, watching and praying that we will follow the right way. Matthew 26:41 says:

> Watch and pray, that ye enter not into temptation: the spirit indeed is willing, but the flesh is weak.

Thought Thirty-six
LIGHT TO JUDGE BY

We are given the light of Christ which is truth whereby we may judge correctly. Moroni 7:18 says:

> And now, my brethren, seeing that ye know the light by which ye may judge, which light is the light of Christ, see

that ye do not judge wrongfully; for with that same judgment which ye judge ye shall also be judged.

There is a misconception that it is more righteous to follow without question.

But as the host that followed Satan found out, ignorance is captivity not righteousness.

Our brothers and sisters were lost even before this world was, because they followed in ignorance.

Truth and agency are not only the mandate for our very existence, but our progress.

Can we give it away, and not expect the same consequences that Satan and his hosts suffered?

Thought Thirty-seven
SYMBOLIC REMINDER

Because of the great significance of the loss of Satan and his hosts, there is a symbolic reminder.

Every time it storms with lightning and rain, we can be reminded. Luke 10:18 says:

And he said unto them, I beheld Satan as lightning fall from heaven.

D&C 76:26 says:

And was called Perdition, for the heavens wept over him—he was Lucifer, a son of the morning.

The lightning symbolizes the dramatic fall of our many brothers and sisters from heaven in a flash as their last bit of light is lost.

The rain reminds us of the tears of sorrow we shed for their great loss of agency, truth and light.

The Lord needs us to protect our agency and to return to Him. He has already lost enough.

Thought Thirty-eight
SUFFICIENT TRUTH

If we haven't taught sufficient truth to those within our influence and are afraid to give them their free agency, they may pull away from us.

At this point we haven't understood free agency any better than Satan and his host of followers.

Truth is power to govern oneself righteously. We can force no one successfully.

Just as our Father in Heaven had to allow one of His great sons to fall, taking with him one-third of His kingdom, we, also, have to allow everyone to make their own decisions.

We should, however, be sure that we have done our best to teach all the truth possible upon which to base those decisions.

We should give them sufficient freedom from ignorance in which to grow. Proverbs 22:6 says:

> Train up a child in the way he should go: and when he is old, he will not depart from it.

In teaching correct principles we have set the right course to freedom and progress and now we must allow all to follow if they will.

WHAT ARE THE PRINCIPLES OF INTELLIGENCE?

———————

A middle-aged man felt that his "knowledge and living to the letter of the law" of the gospel qualified him as superior in righteousness. He arrogantly put down the humble and unlearned in any and all circumstances in which he found himself. As a father of a Scout, he brow beat the Scoutmaster with the text book on Scouting. In Gospel Doctrine class he put "his" interpretations as the only acceptable ones. Did he really have any principles of intelligence, or just knowledge?

Thought Thirty-nine

MISUNDERSTOOD INTELLIGENCE

We are intelligences and we are to increase in that intelligence. D&C 130:18-19 says:

> Whatever principle of intelligence we attain unto in this life, it will rise with us in the resurrection. And if a person gains more knowledge and intelligence in this life through his diligence and obedience than another, he will have so much the advantage in the world to come.

This scripture has been misunderstood to mean, the more secular education we obtain in this life, the further we will go in the life to come. 3 Nephi 6:12 says:

> And the people began to be distinguished by ranks, according to their riches and their chances for learning; yea, some were ignorant because of their poverty, and others did receive great learning because of their riches.

What of the poor? Would they have as much chance to progress in the kingdom of God as the rich?

Consider for a moment Christ, or Joseph Smith, who were both poor according to secular educations and the things of the world.

Where would they be if this were true?

———◆———

Thought Forty

WHAT OF SECULAR KNOWLEDGE?

Though secular knowledge has it's place, it isn't necessary for exaltation. It isn't that kind of knowledge that will increase our eternal intelligence. D&C 38:26 says:

> For what man among you having twelve sons, and is no respecter of them, and they serve him obediently, and he saith unto the one: Be thou clothed in robes and sit thou here; and to the other: Be thou clothed in rags and sit thou there—and looketh upon his sons and saith I am just?

If the Lord is indeed just, and we know He is, then these kinds of educations are not prerequisite to progressing in the kingdom of God.

After all, we lived in the pre-existence for thousands of years, and during that time we were not kept in a vacuum.

We were continually learning. We could read, write, speak languages, play musical instruments and more.

Much of what we learn here in schools, we knew already. We've just forgotten it for this life.

So, if it has eternal relevance, it will work for all, both rich and poor, because we all received it in the pre-existence. D&C 138:56 says:

> Even before they were born, they, with many others, received their first lessons in the world of spirits and were prepared to come forth in the due time of the Lord to labor in his vineyard for the salvation of the souls of men.

Thought Forty-one
WHICH KNOWLEDGE SHOULD BE SOUGHT?

1 Corinthians 13:2 says:

> And though I have...all knowledge;...

The knowledge we should be seeking here can only be found in application of character-building truths.

We came to this world to prove ourselves worthy of returning with the *intelligence that has eternal influence.*

The spiritual knowledge and secular education that gives us advantage in the world to come has it's relevance in making our characters celestial.

As we increase our understanding of the doctrine and what it requires of us, we increase our ability to apply and live it more fully.

Understanding doctrine correctly is knowledge. Knowledge, applied properly, equates to principles of intelligence obtained.

These have the everlasting advantages promised in the D&C 130:18-19 which says:

> Whatever principle of intelligence we attain unto in this life, it will rise with us in the resurrection. And if a person gains more knowledge and intelligence in this life through his diligence and obedience than another, he will have so much the advantage in the world to come.

GREATER UNDERSTANDING

D&C 130:18-19 says:

> Whatever principle of intelligence we attain unto in this life, it will rise with us in the resurrection. And if a person gains more knowledge and intelligence in this life through his diligence and obedience than another, he will have so much the advantage in the world to come.

To understand this scripture in it's correct perspective, we must take a closer look.

The key words, if understood, will unlock the meaning. (Webster's dictionary was used for this purpose.)

We start with *attain unto* which means to *make our own.*

So whatever *principle of intelligence we make our own,* will rise with us in the resurrection.

Diligence means *continual devotion* and *obedience* means *submission to knowledge.*

So, if a person makes more knowledge and intelligence *their own* in this life *through his continual devotion and submission to that knowledge,* than another, he will have so much the advantage in the world to come.

Thought Forty-three
IS THERE MORE TO INTELLIGENCE?

There is more to intelligence. 1 Corinthians 13:2 says:

> And though I have the gift of prophecy, and understand all mysteries, and *all knowledge;*…and have not charity, *I am nothing.*

With knowledge alone we are nothing.

It says that it must be knowledge fused with charity in order to benefit us.

This is true intelligence and knowledge that will advance us in the world to come.

Making knowledge into a principle of intelligence is what *making it our own* means.

As we obtain true intelligence, the ultimate effect in character is our assurance that we have implemented the doctrine correctly in our lives.

Thought Forty-four
WHAT MAKES OUR WORKS VALID?

1 Corinthians 13:3 says:

> And though I bestow all my goods to feed the poor, and though I give my body to be burned, and have not charity, *it profiteth me nothing.*

Our gifts and doing good works must incorporate charity if they are to profit us.

This is the works of intelligence that will give us furtherance in the kingdom of God, or added glory.

So what is charity? In 1 Corinthians 13:4-8, Paul describes it this way:

> Charity suffereth long, and is kind, charity envieth not; charity vaunteth not itself, is not puffed up, Doth not behave itself unseemly, seeketh not her own, is not easily provoked, thinketh no evil; rejoiceth not in iniquity, but

rejoiceth in the truth; Beareth all things, believeth all things hopeth all things, endureth all things. Charity never faileth; but whether there be prophecies, they shall fail; whether there be tongues they shall cease; whether there be *knowledge*, it shall *vanish away*.

Gaining charity is gaining quality of character or the person we have become.

Knowledge, when not applied and worked into intelligence, *vanishes away*, and our talents and gifts *fail*.

Thought Forty-five
HOW DOES IT WORK?

A principle of intelligence obtained, equals a change of heart. 2 Corinthians 4:6 says:

> For God, who commanded the light to shine out of darkness, *hath shined in our hearts, to give light of the knowledge of the glory of God in the face of Jesus Christ.*

If our hearts, which are worldly and selfish, change little by little, or line upon line, precept upon precept, into hearts full of charity, then we gain higher levels of intelligence which gives us the advantage in the life to come.

But if we just have the *knowledge*, and not the *spirit* of Christ shining through our heart it *profiteth us nothing*. 1 Timothy 1:5 says:

> Now the end of the commandment is charity out of a pure heart, and of a good conscience, and of faith unfeigned;

The end result of obedience to the commandments is obtaining *charity* or making Christ shine through our hearts. Moroni 7:47 says:

> But charity is the pure love of Christ, and it endureth forever and whoso is found possessed of it at the last day, it shall be well with him.

True charity is *intelligence* which we possess when we have the pure love of Christ.

Thought Forty-six
MORE SCRIPTURES

The scripture in John 8:31 is an endorsement of the scripture in D&C 130:18-19. They both say we have true intelligence through correct application of the word or knowledge. John 8:31 says:

> Then said Jesus to those Jews which believed on him, *If ye continue in my word,* then are ye my disciples *indeed;*

To *continue* means to *persevere* or *persist,* and *in* means *to engage* or *act upon,* and *indeed* can have a double meaning, both very applicable.

One meaning is *in actuality* and the other is *in the deed* meaning *in the actions or behavior.*

So the scripture says, if we *persevere* or *persist acting upon* the word, then we are Christ's disciples *in actuality, in deeds, and behavior.*

When our hearts are changed through the process of gaining *true intelligence,* or the pure love of Christ, and it is evidenced through our benevolent behavior, then we can understand even better. D&C 93:36-37:

> The glory of God is intelligence, in other words, light and truth. Light and truth forsake that evil one.

Our *true intelligence* or pure love of Christ, is glory as in "Celestial kingdom glory."

Thought Forty-seven
EXAMINE OURSELVES

Since we will be examined by the Lord at judgment, it is wise for us to consistently examine ourselves and the truths we apply or don't apply through Christ.

Socrates taught:

> That life which is unexamined is not worth living.

2 Corinthians 13:5 says:

> Examine yourselves, whether ye be in the faith; prove your ownselves.

Where do we stand in regard to these principles of intelligence or glory?

The understanding of what true intelligence is facilitates the answer, thus enabling us to work at obtaining it.

It frees us from ignorance and brings us more in line with a God-like nature or, in other words, we increase in glory. John 8:32 says:

> And ye shall know the truth and the truth shall make you free.

Part Two

GAINING SPIRITUAL POWERS

How Do I Gain Humility for Spiritual Power?

Is Peace Spiritual Power?

Is There Spiritual Power in Knowledge?

WHAT IS GIVEN?

In an institute class a young woman learned how Satan still knew and remembered everyone and everything about the pre-existence which she had been made to forget.

To think that Satan knew who she and her mission were, even better than she herself knew, disturbed her greatly. She felt that this gave Satan an unfair advantage over her.

Were there any advantages given to her by a loving Heavenly Father?

Thought Forty-eight
BE THOU GOD-WARD

We can realize how much our Father in Heaven is watching over us if we read the scriptures.

One of these scriptures is found in Hebrews 13:5 which says:

> ...for He hath said, I will never leave thee, nor forsake thee.

Another scripture in Exodus 18:18-20 not only tells us that we are not able to do it alone, but how we are to receive the help we are promised above. It says:

> Thou wilt surely wear away, both thou, and this people that is with thee: for this thing is too heavy for thee; thou art not able to perform it thyself alone. Hearken now unto my voice, I will give thee counsel, and God shall be with thee: Be thou for the people to *God ward:* And thou shalt teach them ordinances and laws, and shalt shew them the way wherein they must walk, and the work that they must do.

Here Jethro, Moses' father-in-law, was instructing Moses to take the peoples' problems to God.

We are given prayer as a way to gain the help we need from Heavenly Father.

Heavenly Father has never left us alone, especially in our becoming like Him and gaining victory over this life.

Thought Forty-nine
THE LIGHT OF CHRIST

Our intelligence or degree of truth and light, which we came into the world with, is not sufficient alone for us to be victorious in this life.

We are still just little glories, who can't withstand the element of darkness that is given as opposition. Ephesians 5:12 says:

> For we wrestle not against flesh and blood, but against principalities, against powers, against the rulers of the

darkness of this world, against spiritual wickedness in high places.

For this reason, God added the Light of Christ to our own for strength sufficient to succeed. John 1:9 says:

> That was the true Light, which lighteth every man that cometh into the world.

Also D&C 88:50 says:

> Then shall ye know that ye have seen me, that I am, and that I am the true light that is in you, and that you are in me; otherwise ye could not abound.

Thought Fifty
DANGER OF MISJUDGING

Because of the opposition in all things, we need to judge right from wrong and good from evil. On our own we cannot do this. Moroni 7:14 says:

> Wherefore, take heed, my beloved brethren, that ye do not judge that which is evil to be of God, or that which is good and of God to be of the devil.

So we are not only given the light of Christ whereby we may abound, but by which we may also judge correctly. The Light of Christ is Truth. Moroni 7:18 says:

> And now, my brethren, seeing that ye know the light by which ye may judge, which light is the light of Christ, see that ye do not judge wrongfully; for with that same judgment which ye judge ye shall also be judged.

There is a real danger of misjudging if we lean to our own understanding, and it could be spiritually fatal.

Thought Fifty-one
GIFTS OF THE SPIRIT

In order to help us in our life's work we were given certain spiritual gifts. Maybe it was the gift of faith, or discernment, or one of many others.

We don't have to work for these—just like the light of Christ, they are given to us. D&C 46:11-12 says:

> For all have not every gift given unto them; for there are many gifts, and to every man is given a gift by the Spirit of God. To some is given one, and to some is given another, that all may be profited thereby.

Though they are given to us, we must not take them for granted. It is essential to magnify and use them *that all may be profited thereby*, as well as to strive to obtain more.

If we do not magnify them they will be taken from us. Remember the outcome of the parable of the talents?

———

Thought Fifty-two
WHAT CAN WE LEARN?

The parable of the talents can teach us why we should magnify talents. Matthew 25:15-21 records this parable.

> And unto he gave five talents, to another two, and to another one:…Then he that had received the five talents went and traded with the same, and made them other five talents. And likewise he that had received two, he also gained other two. But he that had received one went and digged in the earth, and hid his lord's money. After a long time the lord of those servants cometh, and reckoneth with them.

The Lord was pleased with the first two servants who had increased their talents. And—

> [Their] lord said unto (them), Well done, thou good and faithful servant(s); thou hast been faithful over a few things, I will make thee ruler[s] over many things; enter thou into the joy of thy lord.

But the one that received one talent, and buried it, had quite a different experience. Matthew 25:24-28 tells of his fate. It says:

> Then he which had received the one talent came and said, Lord, I knew thee that thou art an hard man,...I was afraid, and went and hid thy talent in the earth: Lo, there thou hast that is thine. His lord answered and said unto him, Thou wicked and slothful servant,...Take therefore the talent from him, and give it unto him which hath ten talents.

Thought Fifty-three
GOD POWERS

In our second estate we have opportunities for increasing our intelligence or glory, just as we did in the first estate.

However, this estate has different conditions from the first.

Here we are no longer in a spiritual existence where we had the constant presence of our Father in Heaven and brother Jesus Christ.

Our separation from them is predicated on the physical laws which govern this progressive experience.

Because it is a physical state, the progress we make must satisfy physical laws.

For this we were given more than the light of Christ and the gifts of the spirit—we were given God-Powers.

The power to procreate is one, given to women, and shared with men.

Also, the Priesthood, or power of God to govern and execute essential physical ordinances, was given to men, and shared with women. Genesis 3:17 says:

> Unto the woman he said, I will greatly multiply thy sorrow and thy conception; in sorrow *thou shalt bring forth children;* and thy desire shall be to thy husband, and *he shall rule over thee.*

The ordinances that are implemented by the priesthood, and having children are physical evidence of obedience.

THE PLAN OF MERCY

We must satisfy both physical and spiritual laws in order to progress.

One of these laws which must be satisfied is justice. Christ's atonement, his physical death, resurrection and spiritually taking upon Himself our sins, satisfies the laws of justice. In this, He balanced justice with mercy.

However, there are physical and spiritual prerequisites to claiming this atonement.

We must accept Christ, take His name upon ourselves and be baptized.

This is where Priesthood power enables us to utilize the power of the atonement.

Without the Priesthood to validate the ordinances, the atonement couldn't release us from our sins, and the eternal impact would be devastating. Alma 42:15 says:

> And now, the plan of mercy could not be brought about except an atonement should be made; therefore God himself atoneth for the sins of the world, to bring about the plan of mercy, to appease the demands of justice, that God might be a perfect, just God, and a merciful God also.

However, because there was an atonement, ordinances accessed through the priesthood can show physical progress, but are not the ultimate evidence of obedience.

Our hearts must be changed by these physical actions in order to show spiritual progress.

Thought Fifty-five
KNOWLEDGE FOR PROGRESS

Our Heavenly Father knows as weak and imperfect as we are, not having sufficient light, truth, intelligence or glory to overcome the world, we need to increase in knowledge.

Knowledge is fundamental in accomplishing our particular missions in life.

Heavenly Father provided this knowledge through His prophets who have all kept records.

We have the Bible, Book of Mormon, the Doctrine and Covenants and the Pearl of Great Price. In these we have been given knowledge. Without knowledge there is no progress.

Of course knowledge without correct application *vanishes away* so we must not only gain it, but live by it. D&C 98:11 says:

> And I give unto you a commandment, that ye shall forsake all evil and cleave unto all good, that ye shall live by every word which proceedeth forth out of the mouth of God.

Also the Lord has given us a living Prophet on the earth today. Through him we may receive even further knowledge through modern-day revelation.

———◆———

Thought Fifty-six
CHRIST IS OUR FOUNDATION

The level of intelligence we obtain depends upon our own compliance to God and His will. 1 Corinthians 3:10-17 says:

> According to the grace of God which is given unto me, as a wise master builder, I have laid the foundation, and another buildeth thereon. But let every man take heed how he buildeth thereupon. For other foundation can no man lay than that is laid, which is Jesus Christ. Now if any man build upon this foundation gold, silver, precious stones, wood, hay, stubble; Every man's work shall be made manifest: for the day shall declare it, because it shall be revealed

by fire; and the fire shall try every man's work of what sort it is. If any man's work abide which he hath built thereupon, he shall receive a reward. If any man's work shall be burned, he shall suffer loss: but he himself shall be saved; yet so as by fire. Know ye not that ye are the temple of God and that the Spirit of God dwelleth in you? If any man defile the temple of God, him shall God destroy; for the temple of God is holy, which temple ye are.

We add to our intelligence, or build upon the *foundation* of God's temple which is *Christ,* for we have His *light* within us.

We, being the temple, or the house of the spirit of God, and *glory*—are holy, and must not defile ourselves.

———◆———

Thought Fifty-seven

WE ARE THE KINGDOM OF GOD

The *kingdom* of God is degrees of glory or intelligence, light and truth. We are intelligences and intelligence is the glory of God, so the *kingdom* of God is in us. Luke 17:20-21 says:

And when he was demanded of the Pharisees, when the kingdom of God should come, he answered them and said, The kingdom of God cometh not with observation: Neither shall they say, Lo here! or lo there! for, behold, the kingdom of God is within you.

Yet we are not completely submissive to the will of the Lord, or in other words, perfect, so we must grow line upon line, precept upon precept until we are complete. D&C 98:12 says:

For he will give unto the faithful line upon line, precept upon precept; and I will try you and prove you herewith.

———◆———

Thought Fifty-eight
THE THREE DEGREES OF INTELLIGENCE

Whatever level of glory or intelligence we work to obtain, there will be a place for us in the hereafter, which is why there are three degrees of glory or levels of *intelligence*. D&C 76:70-71, 81 says:

> These are they whose bodies are celestial, whose glory is that of the sun, even the glory of God, the highest of all,...And again, we saw the terrestrial world,...these are they whose glory differs from that of the church of the Firstborn who have received the fullness of the Father, even as that of the moon differs from the sun in the firmament. And again, we saw the glory of the telestial, which glory is that of the lesser, even as the glory of the stars differs from that of the glory of the moon in the firmament.

The three degrees of glory help us better understand what is expected of us when we are told to become perfect even as our Father in heaven is perfect.

Thought Fifty-nine
GOD HAS GIVEN US ALL

It is acknowledging that God has given us everything to fulfill our purpose in life, progressing unto perfection which inspires proclamations like the following in 2 Corinthians 7:1:

> Having therefore these promises, dearly beloved, let us cleanse ourselves from all filthiness of the flesh and spirit, perfecting holiness in the fear of God.

When we are moved by all He has given and promised already, we will be obedient and cleanse ourselves from the world.

After which, we can put our knowledge to work to gain greater levels of *intelligence* or *glory*, and become like Him, regaining His presence. D&C 88:107 says:

And then shall the angels be crowned with the glory of his might and the saints shall be filled with his glory, and receive their inheritance and be made equal with him.

HOW DOES FASTING INCREASE OUR SPIRITUAL POWER?

An older sister was known for her spiritual power and the strength with which she would render her prayers and service to the Lord.

What most people didn't know was that she not only fasted on Fast Sunday each month, but also fasted occasionally when trials would come upon her.

She was constantly increasing in her faith and companionship with the Lord. Do we need to be commanded in all things? How can fasting increase our spiritual power?

Thought Sixty
FASTING AND SPIRITUAL POWER

Knowledge and application of the *principle* of fasting helps us gain the principle of faith necessary for overcoming Satan and obtaining exaltation.

Fasting looses ourselves from everything earthly which could prohibit our hearts from being focused singley to God. Isaiah 58:6-7 says:

> Is not this the fast that I have chosen? to lose the bands of wickedness, to undo the heavy burdens and to let the oppressed go free, and that ye break every yoke?

The blessings reaped over and above the loosing of the bands of wickedness, and the unifying of our spirits with our Heavenly Father are given. Isaiah 58:8 says:

> Then shall thy light break forth as the morning, and thine health shall spring forth speedily: and thy right-eousness shall go before thee; the glory of the Lord shall be thy rereward.

A true fast is spiritually, temporally and emotionally working to come closer to God. Daniel 9:3 says:

> And I set my face unto the Lord God, to seek by prayer and supplications, with fasting,...

———◆———

Thought Sixty-one
THE PHYSICAL FAST

The exclusionary element of the physical or temporal fast is the abstinence from food, drink and other physical pleasures.

We enjoin our fast with the Sabbath and abstain also from work or activities that would distract us from centering on the Lord. Isaiah 58:13 says this about the keeping of the Sabbath day:

> ...if thou turn away thy foot from the sabbath, from doing thy pleasure on my holy day; and call the sabbath a

delight, the holy of the lord, honorable; and shalt honour him, not doing thine own ways,...

A physical fast is also an inclusionary experience.

It will include the feeding of the poor and needy, visiting the sick and afflicted, and in general seeing to the needs of the less fortunate. This is partially accomplished by our fast offerings. Isaiah 58:6-7 says:

Is not this the fast that I have chosen? Is it not to deal thy bread to the hungry and that thou bring the poor that are cast out to thy house? when thou seest the naked that thou cover him; and that thou hide not thyself from thine own flesh?

A true fast must have both the exclusionary and inclusionary aspects to be acceptable to the Lord.

———◆———

Thought Sixty-two
THE EMOTIONAL FAST

The emotional part of the fast would exclude secular or worldly interest, such as reading novels, watching secular TV programs, and visiting with others in a jovial, profane manner.

In other words, partaking of or participating in an emotionally feasting atmosphere.

It could include the reading of scriptures or self improvement books, listening to uplifting and peace inducing music, and pondering upon the Savior. Psalms 69:10 says:

When I wept and chastened my soul with fasting.

Weeping and chastening our souls with fasting brings our spirits peace in the Lord through which self control can increase.

Through this introspection which unites us peacefully with the Lord we gain greater emotional clarity and control.

———◆———

Thought Sixty-three
THE SPIRITUAL FAST

The spiritual fast is an inward journey seeking the Lord in prayer and bearing of testimonies in our sacrament meetings.

These testaments would exclude speaking about things or activities that gratify pride which pursues self-aggrandizement, such as boasting on one's own or family accomplishments or trips. Isaiah 58:13-14 in part says:

> ...nor finding thine own pleasure, nor speaking thine own words: Then shalt thou delight thyself in the Lord:...

More importantly they would include testifying of the goodness of the Savior and of spiritual victories obtained through Him.

This increases the spiritual awareness of others to the Savior's work among His people, giving edification to all.

This part of the fast is also for requesting and obtaining forgiveness from the Lord and people against whom we have transgressed, thus increasing in humility. Daniel 9:3-5 says:

> And I set my face unto the Lord God, to seek by prayer and supplications, with fasting, and sackcloth, and ashes: and I prayed unto the Lord my God, and made my confession, and said, O God,...We have sinned and committed iniquity, and have done wickedly, and have rebelled, even by departing from thy precepts and from thy judgments:

Thought Sixty-four
ACCEPTABLE EXCEPTIONS

Combing the physical, emotional and spiritual would be the *ideal* fast under normal circumstances.

However, there are those who, through no fault of their own cannot go without food for any prolonged period of time.

In these cases it is proper to substitute the *abstinence* of food, for food prepared and eaten with a singleness of heart. D&C 59:13 says:

> And on this day thou shalt do none other thing, only let thy food be prepared with singleness of heart that thy fasting may be perfect, or in other words, that thy joy may be full.

The older person, young children, or physically challenged persons may need a certain amount of food on this day to prevent serious health difficulties.

In such cases the simpleness in which the food is prepared does not interfere with the spiritual purposes or *principle* of fasting, which is *singleness of heart.*

Remember the principle of the fast, or purpose is not to go without food. It is to break the hold the world has on our minds and hearts. Joel 2:12 says:

> Therefore also now, saith the Lord, turn ye even to me with all your heart, and with fasting, and with weeping, and with mourning.

Thought Sixty-five
OTHER PRINCIPLES

Other principles can be used in deciding how a healthy and effective fast may be performed. In Mosiah 4:27 in part says:

> And see that all these things are done in wisdom and order; for it is not requisite that man should run faster than he has strength...

The principle of not doing more than we have strength to accomplish is also applicable to our fasting. Also in Mosiah 4:24-25 it says:

> And again, I say unto the poor, ye who have not and yet have sufficient, that ye remain from day to day; I mean all you who deny the beggar, because ye have not; I would that ye say in your hearts that: I give not because I have not, but if I had I would give. And now, if ye say this in your hearts ye remain guiltless,...

The same principle that applies in not giving because we *have not* applies in the *principle* of the fast.

If we say in our hearts, *I abstain not from food because I cannot, but I would abstain if I could.*—then we will also be found guiltless, and our fast will be respected and acceptable to the Lord as a perfect fast.

KING NEBUCHADNEZZAR'S FAST

If we remember the true purposes or *principles* of the fast, which are:

To focus our whole selves upon our Father in heaven and increase our spiritual *integrity* in calling down blessings:

We can then understand why the fast that king Nebuchadnezzar held for Daniel was effective even though his fast did not exclude eating.

It only withheld him from normal physical gratification of music and sleep. It consisted of devoting himself entirely to prayer in behalf of Daniel. Daniel 6:18 says:

> Then the king went to his palace, and passed the night fasting: neither were instruments of musick brought before him: and his sleep went from him.

Whether it was his fasting or Daniel's faithfulness or a combination of both that brought the blessing of safety is not clear.

However king Nebuchadnezzar's fast was sincere and brought about the purpose of total spiritual focus.

MORE BENEFITS OF THE KING'S FAST

King Nebuchadnezzar's fasting not only helped to save Daniel's life, it also humbled his spirit, since it was pride that had caused him to listen to wicked men.

The fast also cleared his mind as to what to do with those men who had wickedly used him to destroy Daniel. Daniel 6:24 says:

> And the king commanded, and they brought those men which had accused Daniel, and they cast them into the den of lions, them, their children, and their wives; and the lions had the master of them, and brake all their bones in pieces...

It accomplished one other thing, which was the complete conversion of king Nebuchadnezzar to the true and living God. Daniel 6:26 records:

> I make a decree, That in every dominion of my kingdom men tremble and fear before the God of Daniel: for he is the living God, and steadfast forever, and his kingdom that which shall not be destroyed, and his dominion shall be even unto the end.

———————

Thought Sixty-eight
THE SIGNIFICANCE OF FASTING

The *principle* of fasting is one of the most powerful act we can make in showing Heavenly Father our sincerity and devotion.

It gives us spiritual power to communicate directly with the Father of our spirits, and call down blessings from heaven.

When we are confused in our important decisions, or in need of a special blessing of any kind, fasting can add strength and focus to our prayers.

It weakens the hold the world has on our minds and hearts, as it breaks the bands that hold us to our worldly pursuits.

Every righteous people recorded have been found to be a people of fasting and prayer.

Such a people were found among the inhabitants of ancient America after the visit of the Savior. 4 Nephi 1:12 says:

> ...but they did walk after the commandments which they had received from their Lord and their God, continuing in

fasting and prayer, and in meeting together oft both to pray and to hear the word of the Lord.

———————

Thought Sixty-nine
A Right and Wrong Way

Of course, as in everything, there is a true way and false way.

The Pharisees were known to fast, but they fasted to be seen of men. Luke 18:11-12 says:

> The Pharisee stood and prayed thus with himself, God, I thank thee, that I am not as other men are, extortioners, unjust, adulterers, or even as this publican. I fast twice in a week, I give tithes of all that I possess.

The Savior expounded upon the true principle of the fast when He said let thy fasting be in secret. 3 Nephi 13:5, 16-18 says:

> ...Moreover, when ye fast be not as the hypocrites, of a sad countenance, for they disfigure their faces that they may appear unto men to fast. Verily I say unto you they have their reward. But thou, when thou fastest, anoint thy head, and wash thy face that thou appear not unto men to fast, but unto thy Father who is in secret; and thy Father who seeth in secret, shall reward thee openly.

———————

Thought Seventy
An Illustration of Pride

There is a story that illustrates the importance of focusing our performance of an ordinance like fasting on its *purpose.*

> A sister who had diabetes came to Church every Sunday with food that she might eat at the appropriate times in order to keep her health. On fast Sunday she got up and said, that due to her health she could not fast, and would

the sisters please consider their fasts as her fast. She wanted them to perform her fast by proxy.

This is right for *ordinances* that are physically performed works for the dead because they are incapable of doing their own, but *principles* are a work of the inner spirit, and cannot be performed by others for us.

Psalms 35:13 says:

...I humbled my soul with fasting;...

Humility is one of the benefits that comes from true fasting. We cannot gain humility for anyone but ourselves.

At first a friend thought she didn't understand the principles of fasting, so she gave her some basic information.

However, instead of being grateful for this information, she was resentful. Not only had she not understood that she could still fast, but she wanted to display her disability and receive honor for her suffering.

The friend had inadvertantly taken that away.

❦

HOW DO I GAIN HUMILITY FOR SPIRITUAL POWER?

———◆———

A young missionary spending a week at the old mission home in Salt Lake City, Utah found that his gift of a photographic memory helped him memorize the first discussion without the help of clue words.

However, when he took his memorized discussion to the returned missionary in charge of passing off the discussions, he was told that unless he used the clue words he could not pass it off.

The young missionary explained that because of his gift he didn't need these clue words, and that they interfered with the process.

The returned missionary abruptly told him that he was not humble and would therefore be a total failure on his mission.

In all actuality, wasn't it the returned missionary who lacked humility in not allowing the great gift, which this young missionary had, to be magnified in the Lord's work?

Thought Seventy-one
WHAT IS HUMILITY?

1 Corinthians 13:4 says:

> ...vaunteth not itself, is not puffed up,...

Humility is a principle of intelligence or glory.

It is a celestial quality of character that will further us in the pursuit of all other principles of glory or intelligence.

Humility is the spiritual balancer that keeps all of our spiritual gifts, works and principles of intelligence in the straight and narrow.

It is the one thing which keeps us from extremes in our pursuit for eternal life or in other words, focuses our *faith and hope* in Christ, and not ourselves.

If we exercise faith without humility, we will begin to put too much credence in our own power of *faith.*

If we do many works without humility, we will put too much credence in our own abilities and eliminate *hope* in Christ.

If we gain great knowledge without humility, we will lean to our own understanding. Without humility, charity is impossible.

Thought Seventy-two
THE CLOSER TO GOD

The closer we are to God, and our former relationship with Him, the easier it is to see and be accountable for our carnal weaknesses.

The more we recognize and accept responsibility for them, the greater level of humility we obtain.

There is an account of Moses obtaining the principle of humility. Moses 1:9 says:

> And the presence of God withdrew from Moses, that his glory was not upon Moses; and Moses *was left unto*

himself. And as he was left unto himself, he fell unto the earth.

Moses experienced a profound truth.

When we are left unto ourselves, and our own *glory*, without God, we fall to the earth, both literally and doctrinally by falling into worldly or earthly thinking and habits.

———————

Thought Seventy-three

MAN IS POWERLESS WITHOUT GOD

Moses 1:10 teaches us about the principle of humility by stating:

> And it came to pass that it was the space of many hours before Moses did again receive his natural strength like unto man; and he said unto himself: *Now, for this cause I know that man is nothing, which thing I never had supposed.*

From this experience Moses gained the highest level of this *principle of intelligence of humility.*

As the presence of God withdrew and he fell to the earth, he realized he was nothing without Him.

Remember we are very small intelligences.

Consider a very small baby left without someone to care for it.

Truly it would not grow and develop on its own power; in fact, it would die.

We are like babies, powerless without God.

———————

Thought Seventy-four

FROM WHENCE IT COMES

When we come closer to God, the veil becomes thinner and our eternal perspective clarifies and commences to enlarge our understanding.

So it is through the process of getting closer to God that we are able to see our nothingness, our total dependence on Him, as Moses did.

Until Moses experienced the presence of God and then the withdrawing of it, he never had supposed that he was nothing without God—nor could he.

God lends us our very breath and he created our physical existence, so where can we take credit for anything in this life? 2 Corinthians 4:7 says:

> But we have this treasure in earthen vessels that the excellency of the power may be of God, and not of us.

We are the earthen vessels, our spirits being embodied in clay, and the treasure is the light of Christ that is given to each of us.

The superiority of the power, this light of Christ in us, is of God and not of us.

Thought Seventy-five

HOW TO REMOVE SPIRITUAL BLINDNESS

Mosiah 4:11 says:

> And again I say unto you as I have said before, that as ye have come to the knowledge of the glory of God, or if ye have known of his goodness and have tasted of his love, and have received a remission of your sins, which causeth such exceedingly great joy in your souls, even so I would that ye should remember, and always retain in remembrance, *the greatness of God, and your own nothingness, and his goodness and long suffering towards you, unworthy creatures,* and humble yourselves even in *the depths of humility, calling on the name of the Lord daily,* and standing steadfastly in the faith of that which is to come, which was spoken by the mouth of the angel.

Blindness to our faults, weaknesses, and nothingness is caused by our carnal state.

Though it is very difficult for us to see our own nothing-ness, our weaknesses and need for growth, if we move towards God in our hearts, minds and actions, as described in the above scripture, this blindness or veil begins to vanish.

———◆———

Thought Seventy-six
WHY IS IT SO HARD?

We have defense mechanisms that protect us from infor-mation that makes us feel powerless or unworthy of love.

Jealousy, anger, selfishness, ambition, competition, greed and guilt all cause a kind of blindness or are reactions to blindness.

This in turn causes us to reject insightful visions of truth, taking us further away from God.

The carnal state causes spiritual blindness, and spiritual blindness causes the carnal state.

When we are in the close proximity of God and His love for us, we are able to see our weaknesses without fear of reprisal.

We recognize and accept them without feeling less worthy of love, instead, our feelings of self-worth are enhanced.

In experiencing this closeness to God and His love for us, we are filled with the burning desire to conquer our weaknesses and make them strengths.

———◆———

Thought Seventy-seven
PRIDE CAN KILL

If being closer to God makes us humble through seeing our weaknesses, then it follows that the further away from God we go, the more blind we are to our faults and weak-nesses and more prideful we become. Mosiah 11:27-29 says:

> Now when king Noah had heard of the words which Abinadi had spoken unto the people, he was also wroth;

and he said: Who is Abinadi, that I and my people should be judged of him, or who is the Lord, that shall bring upon my people such great affliction? Now the eyes of the people were blinded; therefore they hardened their hearts against the words of Abinadi, and they sought from that time forward to take him. And king Noah hardened his heart against the word of the Lord, and he did not repent of his evil doings.

Wicked king Noah was one who was prideful and distanced from God.

When he was the furthest away from his God, he couldn't be told of his sins by Abinadi.

Though he only started with pride, it became the vehicle for corrupting his people and ultimately murdering the prophet Abinadi.

Thought Seventy-eight
LEAN NOT

Distancing ourselves from God increases our blindness, making us prone to bad judgment and misunderstandings as well. In Proverbs 3:5-7 it says:

> Trust in the Lord with all thine heart; and lean not unto thine own understanding. In all thy ways acknowledge him, and he shall direct thy paths. Be not wise in thine own eyes; fear the Lord, and depart from evil.

Those that are close to God tend to put little credence in their own experience and wisdom and put the wisdom of God first. Jacob 4:7 says:

> Nevertheless, the Lord God showeth us our weakness that we may know that it is by his grace, and his great condescensions unto the children of men, that we have power to do these things.

Also Ether 12:27 which says:

> And if men come unto me I will show unto them their weaknesses. I give unto men weaknesses that they may be humble; and my grace is sufficient for all men that humble

themselves before me, and have faith in me, then I will make weak things strong unto them.

Thought Seventy-nine
NEPHI'S HUMILITY

2 Nephi 4:15-35 is often referred to as the Psalm of Nephi.

In this Psalm, Nephi is approaching God and being brought to his knees in humility because of insights or understanding of his own weaknesses.

> Nevertheless, notwithstanding the great goodness of the Lord, in showing me his great and marvelous works, my heart exclaimeth: O wretched man that I am! Yea, my heart sorroweth because of my flesh; my soul grieveth because of mine iniquities. I am encompassed about, because of the temptations and the sins which do so easily beset me. And when I desire to rejoice, my heart groaneth because of my sins; nevertheless, I know in whom I have trusted.

The closer he came to God, the more clearly he saw his own need for improvement and the more humble he became.

Thought Eighty
PRAISE AND GREAT BLESSINGS

Because of the nearness to God and His love, he praised the Lord, giving him all the glory and credit in total humility. 2 Nephi 4:20-23 says:

> My God hath been my support; he hath led me through mine afflictions in the wilderness; and he hath preserved me upon the waters of the great deep. He hath filled me with his love, even unto the consuming of my flesh. He hath confounded mine enemies, unto the causing of them to quake before me. Behold, he hath heard my cry by day, and he hath given me knowledge by vision in the night-time.

He tells of the great and marvelous blessings that have attended him because of his closeness to God. 2 Nephi 4:24-25 says:

> And by day have I waxed bold in mighty prayer before him; yea, my voice have I sent up on high; and angels came down and ministered unto me. And upon the wings of his Spirit hath my body been carried away upon exceedingly high mountains. And mine eyes have beheld great things, yea, even too great for man; therefore I was bidden that I should not write them

When we obtain this *principle* of humility, we became totally submissive to the Lord and His will and we admit our weaknesses and complete dependence on Him.

Thought Eighty-one

HEARKEN TO AND PRAISE GOD

Those who have distanced themselves from God, lean on their own wisdom, understanding and experience, relying less on the Lord. 2 Nephi 9:28 says:

> O that cunning plan of the evil one! O the vainness, and the frailties, and the foolishness of men! When they are learned they think they are wise, and they hearken not unto the counsel of God, for they set it aside, supposing they know of themselves, wherefore, their wisdom is foolishness and it profiteth them not. And they shall perish. But to be learned is good if they hearken unto the counsels of God.

As we approach God, gaining humility, we learn that it is He who should be praised and glorified. Mosiah 2:20-21 says:

> ...if you should render all the thanks and praise...to that God who has created you, and has kept and preserved you,...and has granted that ye should live in peace one with another—I say unto you that if ye should serve him who...is preserving you from day to day by lending you breath,...and even supporting you from one moment to another...yet ye would be unprofitable servants.

Our dependence on God for everything becomes increasingly clear as we study scriptural encounters of others with God, and experience close encounters with God for ourselves.

PRAISE CAUSES PRIDE

We see in the writings of the prophets and apostles a constant acknowledgement of God because of their closeness to Him.

Also, as we come closer to God, we acknowledge that all we are, ever hope to be or possess, emanates from Him and His love for us. Psalms 150:6 says:

> ...let everything that hath breath praise the Lord. Praise ye the Lord.

As we come to the realization of our nothingness and God's greatness, we also come to the realization of the futility of accepting from or giving praise to our fellowmen.

We are to love, encourage and appreciate one another in our efforts to follow and serve God, and refrain from glorifying anyone other than God.

The prudence in this, though giving and taking praise is the long standing habit of many of us, is the protection it gives us against pride.

It has a great impact on our ability to obtain and secure the *principle of humility*.

Even Heavenly Father in giving recognition to His son, our Savior, did not say, This is my beloved Son in whom I am proud. He said in Matthew 3:17:

> ...This is my beloved Son in whom I am *well pleased*.

NEVER USE THE WORD "PRIDE"

The words pride and proud are *never* used in the scriptures in a positive light. They are always used to refer to sin.

We can be grateful for, appreciative of, and well pleased in ourselves, and others, but we should not be proud.

Even replacing the phrase, "taking *pride* in my work" can be replaced with, "I will show respect for myself in my work."

For something as unfounded as pride, would we jeopardize acquiring this great *principle of intelligence?*

Christ gave all the praise to God—shouldn't we? John 5:19 says:

> Then answered Jesus and said unto them, Verily, verily, I say unto you, The Son can do nothing of Himself, but what he seeth the Father do: for what things soever he doeth, these also doeth the Son likewise.

Also John 8:50 says:

> And I seek not mine own glory: there is one that seeketh and judgeth.

Once we recognize who and what we are in *relation to God*, then we can move forward.

᠅

IS PEACE SPIRITUAL POWER?

———✦———

A young man stated that anger wasn't a sin, but was a matter of self control like overeating.

However, if it negatively effects our spirit's well being or the well being of others, isn't it spiritually connected and a sin?

What happens to our spiritual powers when we are angry? Is peace spiritual power?

Thought Eighty-four
ABIDING IN PEACE

1 Corinthians 13:5 says in part:

> Charity…is not easily provoked,…

Phillipians 4:7 says:

> And the peace of God, which passeth all understanding, shall keep your hearts and minds through Christ Jesus.

Abiding in peace, despite vexing challenges, is to obtain the *principle* of not being easily provoked.

The Lord told Adam and Eve in Genesis 3:17:

> …cursed shall be the ground for thy sake; in sorrow shalt thou eat of it all the days of thy life.

Ever since, we have had irritations, provocations and challenges that have made getting upset and angry not only natural, but commonplace.

Though it may be *natural*, it is neither desirable, nor wise. Proverbs 14:17 says:

> He that is soon angry dealeth foolishly…

Being angry and dealing foolishly is not only unwise, but an unrighteous attribute of our carnal self enhanced by allowing Satan to have control of our hearts instead of Christ, lacking *charity*.

———

Thought Eighty-five
ANGER IS OF SATAN

Anger causes us to separate from, instead of unite with one another. 3 Nephi 11:29 says:

> For verily, verily I say unto you, he that hath the spirit of contention is not of me, but is of the devil, who is the father of contention, and he stirreth up the hearts of men to contend with anger, one with another.

During this probation on earth, Satan's prime objective is to separate us from God and others.

That is why one of the *doctrines of Christ* is to do away with anger. 3 Nephi 11:30 says:

> Behold, this is not my doctrine, to stir up the hearts of men with *anger,* one against another; but this is my doctrine, that such things should be done away.

Identifying the causes of our anger helps us better understand what we have to do to follow this doctrine.

As we identify the causes and follow the doctrine of doing away with anger, we begin to understand ourselves better.

We commence eliminating unnecessary anger from our lives and by so doing, we gain the first level of this *principle intelligence.*

———————◆———————

Thought Eighty-six

JEALOUSY CAUSES ANGER

Jealousy is a cause of anger. Proverbs 6:34 says:

> For jealousy is the *rage* of a man: therefore he will not spare in the day of vengeance.

Jealousy is a carnal weakness that attacks an unsuspecting heart and takes over.

It has been said that jealousy has been at the root of most all violent crimes. It's what caused Cain to kill Abel. But even before that, jealousy claimed it's victims. Abraham 3:27-28 says:

> And the Lord said; whom shall I send? And one answered like unto the Son of Man: Here am I, send me. And another answered and said: Here am I, send me. And the Lord said: I will send the first. And the second was *angry,* and kept not his first estate; and at that day, many followed after him.

Unfortunately, in this case, more than just Satan was lost to the sin of jealousy. His jealousy propagated into rebellion and many more were lost. Jealousy is a sin. Exodus 20:17 says:

> Though shalt not covet thy neighbor's wife, nor his manservant, nor his maidservant, nor his ox, nor his ass, nor anything that is thy neighbor's.

In allowing our jealousy to control and motivate us to anger we lose our light and increase in transgressions which influence others to do the same.

CONTENTMENT CURES JEALOUSY

Contentment which comes from gratefulness is our defense against jealousy. 1 Timothy 6:6-8 says:

> But godliness with *contentment* is great gain. For we brought nothing into this world, and it is certain we can carry nothing out. And having food and raiment let us be therewith *content*.

We don't have to have many things of this world to find peace and contentment.

In fact we need very little of this world to find these, because peace and contentment are not found in worldly possessions or attainments.

They are found in Christ. John 14:27 says:

> Peace I leave with you, my peace I give unto you: not as the world giveth, give I unto you. Let not your heart be troubled, neither let it be afraid.

GUILT AND ANGER

A carnal weakness which can cause us to be angry is guilt. 2 Nephi 33:5 says:

> And it speaketh harshly against sin, according to the plainness of the truth; wherefore, no man will be angry at the words which I have written save *he shall be of the spirit of the devil.*

Guilt displaces peace within us, making us feel at war with our conscience, and of course when we are contending within ourselves against the spirit, we are already argumentative.

We see the negative in every situation and seek justification for our feelings in altercations with those around us.

Fear is a by-product of guilt, and can further our difficulties if we take counsel from it.

We must work on the disease, which is guilt, not just the symptom, which is anger. If we find guilt is the disease causing our anger, then we must apply the correct cure which is repentance. D&C 64:7 says:

> Nevertheless, he has sinned; but verily I say unto you, I, the Lord forgive sins unto those who confess their sins before me and ask forgiveness, who have not sinned unto death.

The healing forgiveness of the Lord is promised to all who will follow this prescription; then peace both within ourselves and with those around us, can be regained.

———◆———

Thought Eighty-nine

DISAPPOINTMENT AND ANGER

Disappointment is another cause of anger. It is the product of unfounded expectations.

Sometimes we expect more from people than we should. After all, we are agents unto ourselves.

The only ones we can truly put expectations on are ourselves, and our Father in Heaven.

We can expect certain things from ourselves, because we have jurisdiction over ourselves.

We can expect certain things from our Father in Heaven, because He is bound when we do what He says. D&C 82:10 says:

> I, the Lord, am bound when ye do what I say; but when ye do not what I say, ye have no promise.

However, we cannot put a time limit on our expectations of Heavenly Father, because if we do, we will risk being disappointed, and angry.

All things are according to the due time of the Lord.1 Nephi 10:3 says:

> That after they should be destroyed, even that great city Jerusalem, and many be carried away captive into Babylon, *according to the own due time of the Lord, they should return again,...*

EXPECTATIONS OR AN ACCEPTING HEART

If, in place of expecting, we are accepting, we will find disappointment-causing anger isn't a problem. 2 Corinthians 8:12 says:

> For if there be first a willing mind, it is *accepted* according to that a man hath, and not according to that he hath not.

Our minds must be willing, making us receptive and accepting, like a little child. Mosiah 3:19 says:

> For the natural man is an enemy to God, and has been from the fall of Adam, and will be forever and ever, unless he *yields* to the enticings of the Holy Spirit, and putteth off the natural man and becometh a saint through the atonement of Christ the Lord, and becometh as a child, submissive, meek, humble, patient, full of love, *willing* to submit to all things which the Lord seeth fit to inflict upon him, even as a child doth submit to his father.

The quality of acceptance is derived from a spiritual or eternal perspective, a looking beyond this life, to the next.

It is the putting off of the natural, or earth-bound man, which frees us from unrealistic expectations of this life.

Thought Ninety-one

WHO PROMISED A ROSE GARDEN?

The mind set is the key to avoiding unnecessary anger. There's the old saying "I never promised you a rose garden."

Life is full of the undesirable, unwanted, and unexpected. Our expectations are met very seldom and this because life is based on the principles of agency.

We all make choices, and suffer consequences, and sometimes we suffer for others' choices as well as our own.

Accepting these difficulties as part of life make them pass without anger and trauma of spirit. D&C 121:7-8 says:

> My son, peace be unto thy soul; thine adversity and thine afflictions shall be but a small moment; And then if thou endure it well, God shall exalt thee on high; thou shalt triumph over all thy foes.

Thought Ninety-two
IF WE ARE OFFENDED

Many times when we are angry, we may feel that we have cause to be so.

Maybe someone has sinned against us with pure evil intent and full knowledge of what he was doing.

However rather than getting angry, we should feel sorry for them, and pray for them.

Even more when someone has offended us unknowingly, or without intending to, we should endure with love, forgiving and understanding. Matthew 5:22 says:

> But I say unto you, That whosoever is angry with his brother, "without a cause," (not in JST) shall be in danger of the judgment:...

Also when we find that we are offended or disappointed we should go to the offender and make peace. D&C 42:88 says:

> ...if thy brother or sister offend thee, thou shalt take him or her between him or her and thee alone; and if he or she confess thou shalt be reconciled.

Looking to a peaceful outcome helps us to *abide in peace* and gain a greater portion of this *principle of intelligence*.

Thought Ninety-three
SPECIAL HELP

We know that we can be forgiving. However, when those who hurt us with real intent attempt to use our own goodness and forgiving efforts against us, it hurts more.

We have heard this kind of person use the scripture in D&C 64:9 often, which says:

> Wherefore, I say unto you, that ye ought to forgive one another; for he that forgiveth not his brother his trespasses standeth condemned before the Lord; for there remaineth in him the greater sin.

They use it to deflect the focus away from their own sin, to our need to forgive them.

The Lord did tell us to forgive others that have transgressed against us, as the scripture in D&C 64:10 says:

> I, the Lord, will forgive whom I will forgive, but of you it is required to forgive all men.

However, the Lord knew that we would have unrepentant offenders like this and these kinds of experiences, so he provided a way to handle them. D&C 64:11 says:

> And ye ought to say in your hearts—let God judge between me and thee, and reward thee according to thy deeds.

Thought Ninety-four
MORE SPECIAL HELP

Though the Savior expects us to be forgiving, He knows that hurt takes time to heal, so he hasn't put any time limit on us to forgive. However, the sooner the better, for an unforgiving heart is void of *charity*.

He also knew that there must be a point where we could find relief from the obligation of forgiving and unrepentant offender.

He has put a limit on the times someone can hurt us intentionally without repenting and still expect forgiveness. D&C 98:41-45 says:

> And if he trespass against thee and repent not the first time, nevertheless, thou shalt forgive him. And if he trespass against thee the second time, and repent not, nevertheless thou shalt forgive him. And if he trespass against thee the third time, and repent not, thou shalt also forgive him. *But if he trespass against thee the fourth time, thou shalt not forgive him*, but shalt bring these testimonies before the Lord; and they shall not be blotted out until he repent and reward thee four-fold in all things wherewith he has trespassed against thee. And if he do this, thou shalt forgive him with all thine heart; and if he do not this, I, the Lord, will avenge thee of thine enemy an hundred-fold;…

The Lord never leaves us powerless against our enemies. This fact alone can bring us great peace. He has shown us how and what to do to attain the *principle of not being easily provoked*, now it is up to us to do it.

Thought Ninety-five
THE SERMON ON THE MOUNT

The sermon on the mount begins by telling us what the blessings are for the correct *attitude*. Matthew 5:9 says:

> Blessed are the peacemakers: for they shall be called the children of God.

Then he gives us some enlightenment as to what to do to become a peacemaker. Matthew 5:25 & 39-45 says:

> Agree with thine adversary quickly, while thou are in the way with him;…But whosoever shall smite thee on thy right cheek, turn to him the other also. And if any man will sue thee at the law, and take away thy coat, let him have thy cloke also. And whosoever shall compel thee to go a

mile, go with him twain. Ye have heard that it hath been said, Thou shalt love thy neighbour, and hate thine enemy. But I say unto you, Love your enemies, bless them that curse you, do good to them that hate you and pray for them which despitefully use you, and persecute you; That ye may be the children of your Father which is in heaven: for he maketh his sun to rise on the evil and on the good, and sendeth rain on the just and on the unjust.

The Sermon on the Mount not only advocates that we not let ourselves get angry, it brings us to an even higher level.

We are to love, bless, do good to, and pray for our enemies, and though we may think this is only benefitting them, on closer examination, we discover that we have received the change of heart and the peace.

———————

Thought Ninety-six
PAHORAN'S EXAMPLE

The peaceable things can all be lost if we do not stop and consider the damage a seemingly *natural* reaction of anger can cause.

The *principle of intelligence* of not being easily provoked is demonstrated by the Chief Judge Pahoran's perception and response to Moroni's angry and offensive epistle accusing him of withholding help.

The humble Pahoran sees Moroni's anger was spurred by his great love and feelings for his people and their immense sufferings.

He does not respond with anger at the unfounded accusation, but instead, pours out his love and understanding in a most Godly and magnanimous way. Alma 61:2 & 9 say:

...Behold I say unto you Moroni, that I do not joy in your great afflictions, yea, it grieves my soul..And now, in your epistle you have censured me, but it mattereth not; I am not angry, but do rejoice in the greatness of your heart...

Pahoran also had a greatness of heart or *charity*. Proverbs 15:18 says:

> A wrathful man stirreth up strife: but he that is slow to anger appeaseth strife.

Pahoran not only turned the situation away from anger and made peace, but he showed forth great love for Moroni and the others.

Pahoran's achievement of not being easily provoked must be what God wants for us.

Thought Ninety-seven

GREAT ANSWERS IN THE SCRIPTURES

We can search the scriptures and find many examples of our ancient leader's spiritual power gained through peace.

As we read them we will be inspired to lift ourselves to a higher and more gracious state of mind, called *peace*. D&C 88:125 admonishes us to:

> …above all things, clothe yourselves with the bond of charity, as with a mantle, which is the bond of perfectness and *peace*.

To abide in peace through all the vexing challenges is to gain *true intelligence.*

If we follow the admonitions of Christ through the Sermon on the Mount and other scriptures, we can correctly handle all anger and anger-causing situations.

The Lord has not left us without answers for all our circumstances.

He has given us great men of the scriptures who share their experiences with us, which give us great insights in how they successfully handled their anger causing situations.

We too can know how to reach for and abide in peace.

IS THERE SPIRITUAL POWER IN KNOWLEDGE?

An elderly man went to Church regularly, but never read or studied the scriptures on his own. Consequently he never seemed to improve in his knowledge of the Gospel.

Because of this, he would often make comments that were totally inappropriate or misleading about the gospel doctrines.

One day during a discussion with his son he insisted that the story of Daniel in the lion's den was found in the Book of Mormon, not the Bible.

Was he truly spiritually able to grow? Without knowledge can we gain spiritual power?

THE IMPORTANCE OF KNOWLEDGE

Isaiah knew that the lack of knowledge allows the masters to become the slaves, and the slaves to become the masters. Isaiah 5:13 says:

> Therefore my people are gone into captivity, because they have no knowledge: and their honourable men are famished, and their multitude dried up with thirst.

Knowledge is truth and truth makes us free, so the lack of knowledge is captivity.

The honorable men were famished or starving because they lacked knowledge of the bread of life, which is Christ.

When they did not have, through knowledge, the living water which is Christ, the multitudes or people under them were left thirsty. John 6:35 says:

> And Jesus said unto them, I am the bread of life: he that cometh to me shall never hunger; and he that believeth on me shall never thirst.

INVALIDATING THE SAVIOR'S SACRIFICE

We have been given correct principles which we should gain knowledge of and put into practice.

Otherwise we risk being captives of our own ignorance, rendering our Savior's sacrifice invalid. 2 Nephi 2:5 &27 say:

> And men are instructed sufficently that they know good from evil. And the law is given unto men. And by the law no flesh is justified; or by the law men are cut off. Yea, by the temporal law they were cut off and also, by the spiritual law they perish from that which is good and become miserable forever. Wherefore, redemption cometh in and through the Holy Messiah; for he is full of grace and truth…Wherefore,

men are free according to the flesh; and all things are given them which are expedient unto men. And they are free to choose liberty and eternal life, through the great Mediator of all men, or to choose captivity and death, according to the captivity and power of the devil; for he seeketh that all men might be miserable like unto himself.

We can save ourselves from Satan's fate and validate the Savior's sacrifice for us because all things are given which are expedient unto us, such as the knowledge of our Savior and His atoning sacrifice.

Thought One Hundred

KNOWLEDGE IS SPIRITUAL POWER

In the book "The Teachings of the Prophet Joseph Smith" on page 49 it says:

> But we take the liberty (and this we have a right to do) of looking at this order of things...and contrasting it with the order of God as we find in the sacred scriptures. In this review, however, we shall present the points as we consider they were really designed by the Great Giver to be understood, and the happy results arising from a performance of the requirement of heaven as revealed to *everyone* who obeys them; and the consequence attending a false construction, a misrepresentation, or forced meaning that was never designed in the mind of the Lord when He condescended to speak from the heavens to men for their salvation.

We can keep all things in their true perspective for our day in the same manner suggested by Joseph Smith.

We can contrast everything by a study of the sacred scriptures and judge their interpretation according to the results arising from the correct application of true principles.

This insures that there is no misrepresentation or false construction or forced meaning that was never designed in the mind of the Lord.